GIT

Get started with GIT and work with GIT Remote Repository

Adney Ainsley

TABLE OF CONTENTS

INTRODUCTION

GIT is a Version Control System (VCS) (aka Revision Control System (RCS), Source Code Manager (SCM)). A VCS serves as a Repository (or repo) of program codes, including all the historical revisions. It records changes to files at so-called commits in a log so that you can recall any file at any commit point.

WHY VCS?

1. The Repository serves as the backup (in case of code changes or disk crash).
2. It is a living archive of all historical revisions. It lets you revert back to a specific version, if the need arises.
3. It facilitates collaboration between team members, and serves as a project management tool.
4. more...

Git was initially designed and developed by Linus Torvalds, in 2005, to support the development of the Linux kernel.

GIT is a Distributed Version Control System (DVCS). Other popular VCSes include:

1. The standalone and legacy Unix's RCS (Revision Control System).
2. Centralized Client-Server Version Control System (CVCS): CVS (Concurrent Version System), SVN (Subversion) and Perforce.
3. Distributed VCS (DVCS): GIT, Merurial, Bazaar, Darcs.

The mother site for Git is http://git-scm.com.

Setting Up Git

You need to setup Git on your local machine, as follows:

1. Download & Install:

   - For Windows and Mac, download the installer from http://git-scm.com/downloads and run the downloaded installer.
   - For Ubuntu, issue command "sudo apt-get install git".
   - For Windows, use the "Git Bash" command shell bundled with Git Installer to issue commands. For Mac/Ubuntu, use the "Terminal".

2. Customize Git:

Issue "git config" command (for Windows, run "Git Bash" from the Git installed directory. For Ubuntu/Mac, launch a "Terminal"):

```
// Set up your username and email (to be used in
labeling your commits)
$ git config --global user.name "your-name"
$ git config --global user.email "your-
email@youremail.com"
```

The settings are kept in "<GIT_HOME>/etc/gitconfig" (of the GIT installed directory) and "<USER_HOME>/.gitconfig" (of the user's home directory.

You can issue "git config --list" to list the settings:

```
$ git config --list
user.email=xxxxxx@xxxxxx.com
user.name=xxxxxx
```

Git Basics

Git Commands

Git provides a set of simple, distinct, standalone commands developed according to the "Unix toolkit" philosophy - build small, interoperable tools.

To issue a command, start a "Terminal" (for Ubuntu/Mac) or "Git Bash" (for Windows):

```
$ git <command> <arguments>
```

The commonly-used commands are:

1. init, clone, config: for starting a Git-managed project.
2. add, mv, rm: for staging file changes.
3. commit, rebase, reset, tag:
4. status, log, diff, grep, show: show status
5. checkout, branch, merge, push, fetch, pull

HELP AND MANUAL

The best way to get help these days is certainly googling.

To get help on Git commands:

```
$ git help <command>
// or
$ git <command> --help
```

The GIT manual is bundled with the software (under the "doc" directory), and also available online @ http://git-scm.com/docs.

GETTING STARTED WITH LOCAL REPO

There are 2 ways to start a Git-managed project:

1. Starting your own project;

2. Cloning an existing project from a GIT host.

We shall begin with "Starting your own project" and cover "Cloning" later @ "Clone a Project from a Remote Repo".

SETUP THE WORKING DIRECTORY FOR A NEW PROJECT

Let's start a programming project under the working directory called "hello-git", with one source file "Hello.java" (or "Hello.cpp", or "Hello.c") as follows:

```
// Hello.java
public class Hello {
   public static void main(String[] args) {
      System.out.println("Hello, world from GIT!");
   }
}
Compile the "Hello.java" into "Hello.class" (or
"Hello.cpp" or "Hello.c" into "Hello.exe").
```

It is also highly recommended to provide a "README.md" file (a text file in a so-called "Markdown" syntax such as "GitHub Flavored Markdown") to describe your project:

```
// README.md
This is the README file for the Hello-world project.
Now, we have 3 files in the working tree:
"Hello.java", "Hello.class" and "README.md". We do
not wish to track the ".class" as they can be
reproduced from ".java".
```

Initialize a new Git Repo (git init)

To manage a project under Git, run "git init" at the project root directory (i.e., "hello-git") (via "Git Bash" for Windows, or "Terminal" for Ubuntu/Mac):

```
// Change directory to the project directory
$ cd /path-to/hello-git

// Initialize Git repo for this project
$ git init
Initialized empty Git repository in /path-to/hello-
git/.git/

$ ls -al
drwxr-xr-x    1 xxxxx    xxxxx     4096 Sep 14 14:58
.git
-rw-r--r--    1 xxxxx    xxxxx      426 Sep 14 14:40
Hello.class
-rw-r--r--    1 xxxxx    xxxxx      142 Sep 14 14:32
Hello.java
-rw-r--r--    1 xxxxx    xxxxx       66 Sep 14 14:33
README.md
```

A hidden sub-directory called ".git" will be created under your project root directory (as shown in the above "ls -a" listing), which contains ALL Git related data.

Take note that EACH Git repo is associated with a project directory (and its sub-directories). The Git repo is completely contain within the project directory. Hence, it is safe to copy, move or rename the project directory. If your project uses more than one directories, you may create one Git repo for EACH directory, or use symlinks to link up the directories, or ... (?!).

GIT STORAGE MODEL

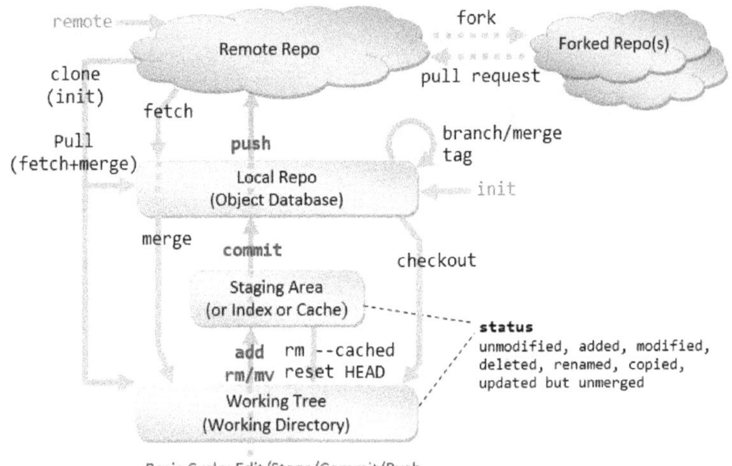

Basic Cycle: Edit/Stage/Commit/Push

The local repo after "git init" is empty. You need to explicitly deposit files into the repo.

Before we proceed, it is important to stress that Git manages changes to files between so-called commits. In other words, it is a version control system that allows you to keep track of the file changes at the commits.

STAGING FILE CHANGES FOR TRACKING (GIT ADD <FILE>...)

Issue a "git status" command to show the status of the files:

```
$ git status
On branch master
Initial commit

Untracked files:
  (use "git add <file>..." to include in what will be
committed)
      Hello.class
      Hello.java
      README.md
nothing added to commit but untracked files present
(use "git add" to track)
```

By default, we start on a branch called "master". We will discuss "branch" later.

In Git, the files in the working tree are either untracked or tracked. Currently, all 3 files are untracked. To stage a new file for tracking, use "git add <file>..." command.

```
// Add README.md file
$ git add README.md

$ git status
On branch master
Initial commit

Changes to be committed:
```

```
  (use "git rm --cached <file>..." to unstage)
        new file:   README.md

Untracked files:
  (use "git add <file>..." to include in what will be
committed)
        Hello.class
        Hello.java

// You can use wildcard * in the filename
// Add all Java source files into Git repo
$ git add *.java

// You can also include multiple files in the "git
add"
// E.g.,
// git add Hello.java README.md

$ git status
On branch master
Initial commit

Changes to be committed:
  (use "git rm --cached <file>..." to unstage)
        new file:   Hello.java
        new file:   README.md

Untracked files:
  (use "git add <file>..." to include in what will be
committed)
        Hello.class
```

The command "git add <file>..." takes one or more filenames or pathnames with possibly wildcards pattern. You can also use "git add ." to add all the files in the current directory (and all sub-directories). But this will include "Hello.class", which we do not wish to be tracked.

When a new file is added, it is staged (or indexed, or cached) in the staging area (as shown in the GIT storage model), but NOT yet committed.

Git uses two stages to commit file changes:

1. "git add <file>" to stage file changes into the staging area, and
2. "git commit" to commit ALL the file changes in the staging area to the local repo.

The staging area allows you to group related file changes and commit them together.

Committing File Changes (git commit)

The "git commit" command commits ALL the file changes in the staging area. Use a -m option to provide a message for the commit.

```
$ git commit -m "First commit"   // -m to specify the
commit message
[master (root-commit) 858f3e7] first commit
 2 files changed, 8 insertions(+)
 create mode 100644 Hello.java
 create mode 100644 README.md

// Check the status
$ git status
On branch master
Untracked files:
  (use "git add <file>..." to include in what will be
committed)
      Hello.class
nothing added to commit but untracked files present
(use "git add" to track)
```

VIEWING THE COMMIT DATA (GIT LOG)

Git records several pieces of metadata for every commit, which includes a log message, timestamp, the author's username and email (set during customization).

You can use "git log" to list the commit data; or "git log --stat" to view the file statistics:

```
$ git log
commit 858f3e71b95271ea320d45b69f44dc55cf1ff794
Author: username <email>
Date:   Thu Nov 29 13:31:32 2012 +0800
    First commit

$ git log --stat
commit 858f3e71b95271ea320d45b69f44dc55cf1ff794
Author: username <email>
Date:   Thu Nov 29 13:31:32 2012 +0800
    First commit
 Hello.java | 6 ++++++
 README.md  | 2 ++
 2 files changed, 8 insertions(+)
```

Each commit is identified by a 40-hex-digit SHA-1 hash code. But we typcially use the first 7 hex digits to reference a commit, as highlighted.

To view the commit details, use "git log -p", which lists all the patches (or changes).

```
$ git log -p
commit 858f3e71b95271ea320d45b69f44dc55cf1ff794
Author: username <email>
Date:   Thu Nov 29 13:31:32 2012 +0800
    First commit
diff --git a/Hello.java b/Hello.java
new file mode 100644
index 0000000..dc8d4cf
--- /dev/null
+++ b/Hello.java
@@ -0,0 +1,6 @@
+// Hello.java
+public class Hello {
+   public static void main(String[] args) {
+      System.out.println("Hello, world from GIT!");
+   }
+}
diff --git a/README.md b/README.md
new file mode 100644
index 0000000..9565113
--- /dev/null
+++ b/README.md
@@ -0,0 +1,2 @@
+// README.md
+This is the README file for the Hello-world project.
```

Below are more options of using "git log":

```
$ git log --oneline
   // Display EACH commit in one line.

$ git log --author="<author-name-pattern>"
   // Display commits by author

$ git log <file-pattern>
   // Display commits for particular file(s)

// EXAMPLES
$ git log --author="Tan Ah Teck" -p Hello.java
   // Display commits for file "Hello.java" by a
particular author
```

FILE STATUS (GIT STATUS)

A file could be untracked or tracked.

As mentioned, Git tracks file changes at commits. In Git, changes for a tracked file could be:

1. unstaged (in Working Tree) - called unstaged changes,
2. staged (in Staging Area or Index or Cache) - called staged changes, or
3. committed (in local repo object database).

The files in "working tree" or "staging area" could have status of unmodified, added, modified, deleted, renamed, copied, as reported by "git status".

The "git status" output is divided into 3 sections: "Changes not staged for commit" for the unstaged changes in "working tree", "Changes to be committed" for the staged changes in the "staging area", and "Untracked files". In each section, It lists all the files that have been changed, i,e., files having status other than unmodified.

When a new file is created in the working tree, it is marked as new in working tree and shown as an untracked file. When the file change is staged, it is marked as new (added) in the staging area, and unmodified in working tree. When the file change is committed, it is marked as unmodified in both the working tree and staging area.

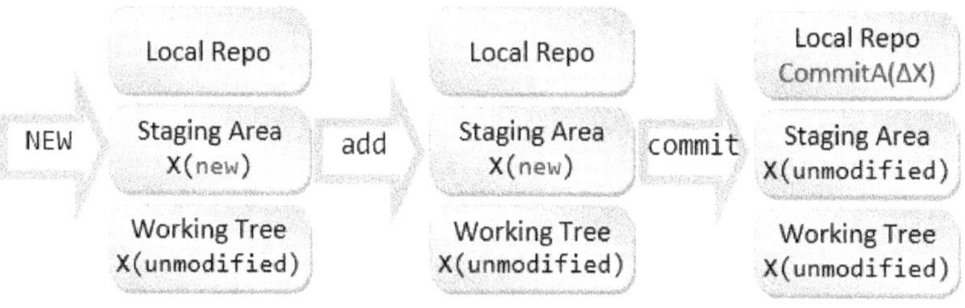

When a committed file is modified, it is marked as modified in the working tree and unmodified in the staging area. When the file change is staged, it is marked as modified in the staging area and unmodified in the working tree. When the file change is committed, it is marked as unmodified in both the working tree and staging area.

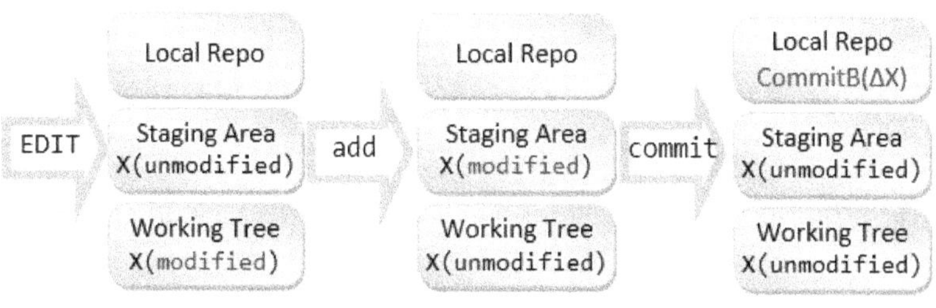

For example, made some changes to the file "Hello.java", and check the status again:

```
// Hello.java
public class Hello {
   public static void main(String[] args) {
      System.out.println("Hello, world from GIT!");
      System.out.println("Changes after First
commit!");
   }
}
```

```
$ git status
On branch master
Changes not staged for commit:
  (use "git add <file>..." to update what will be
committed)
  (use "git checkout -- <file>..." to discard changes
in working directory)
      modified:   Hello.java

Untracked files:
  (use "git add <file>..." to include in what will be
committed)
      Hello.class
no changes added to commit (use "git add" and/or "git
commit -a")
```

The "Hello.java" is marked as modified in the working tree (under "Changes not staged for commit"), but unmodified in the staging area (not shown in "Changes to be committed").

You can inspect all the unstaged changes using "git diff" command (or "git diff <file>" for the specified file). It shows the file changes in the working tree since the last commit:

```
$ git diff
diff --git a/Hello.java b/Hello.java
index dc8d4cf..f4a4393 100644
--- a/Hello.java
+++ b/Hello.java
@@ -2,5 +2,6 @@
 public class Hello {
    public static void main(String[] args) {
       System.out.println("Hello, world from GIT!");
+      System.out.println("Changes after First
commit!");
    }
 }
```

The older version (as of last commit) is marked as --- and new one as +++. Each chunk of changes is delimited by "@@ -<old-line-number>,<number-of-lines> +<new-line-number>,<number-of-lines> @@". Added lines are marked as + and deleted as -. In the above output, older version (as of last commit) from line 2 for 5 lines and the modified version from line 2 for 6 lines are compared. One line (marked as +) is added.

Stage the changes of "Hello.java" by issuing the "git add <file>...":

```
$ git add Hello.java

$ git status
On branch master
Changes to be committed:
  (use "git reset HEAD <file>..." to unstage)
      modified:   Hello.java

Untracked files:
  (use "git add <file>..." to include in what will be
committed)
      Hello.class
```

Now, it is marked as modified in the staging area ("Changes to be committed"), but unmodified in the working tree (not shown in "Changes not staged for commit").

Now, the changes have been staged. Issuing an "git diff" to show the unstaged changes results in empty output.

You can inspect the staged change (in the staging area) via "git diff --staged" command:

```
// List all "unstaged" changes for all files (in the
working tree)
$ git diff
   // empty output - no unstaged change

// List all "staged" changes for all files (in the
staging area)
$ git diff --staged
diff --git a/Hello.java b/Hello.java
index dc8d4cf..f4a4393 100644
--- a/Hello.java
+++ b/Hello.java
@@ -2,5 +2,6 @@
 public class Hello {
    public static void main(String[] args) {
       System.out.println("Hello, world from GIT!");
+      System.out.println("Changes after First
commit!");
    }
 }
   // The "unstaged" changes are now "staged".
```

Commit ALL staged file changes via "git commit":

```
$ git commit -m "Second commit"
[master 96efc96] Second commit
 1 file changed, 1 insertion(+)

$ git status
On branch master
Untracked files:
```

```
  (use "git add <file>..." to include in what will be committed)
      Hello.class
nothing added to commit but untracked files present (use "git add" to track)
```

Once the file changes are committed, it is marked as unmodified in the staging area (not shown in "Changes to be committed").

Both "git diff" and "git diff --staged" return empty output, signalling there is no "unstaged" and "staged" changes.

The stage changes are cleared when the changes are committed; while the unstaged changes are cleared when the changes are staged.

Issue "git log" to list all the commits:

```
$ git log
commit 96efc96f0856846bc495aca2e4ea9f06b38317d1
Author: username <email>
Date:   Thu Nov 29 14:09:46 2012 +0800
    Second commit

commit 858f3e71b95271ea320d45b69f44dc55cf1ff794
Author: username <email>
Date:   Thu Nov 29 13:31:32 2012 +0800
    First commit
```

Check the patches for the latest commit via "git log -p -1", with option -n to limit to the last n commit:

```
$ git log -p -1
commit 96efc96f0856846bc495aca2e4ea9f06b38317d1
Author: username <email>
Date:   Thu Nov 29 14:09:46 2012 +0800
    Second commit
diff --git a/Hello.java b/Hello.java
index dc8d4cf..ede8979 100644
--- a/Hello.java
+++ b/Hello.java
@@ -2,5 +2,6 @@
 public class Hello {
    public static void main(String[] args) {
       System.out.println("Hello, world from GIT!");
+      System.out.println("Changes after First
commit!");
    }
 }
```

I shall stress again Git tracks the "file changes" at each commit over the previous commit.

THE .GITIGNORE FILE

All the files in the Git directory are either tracked or untracked. To ignore files (such as .class, .o, .exe which could be reproduced from source) from being tracked and remove them from the untracked file list, create a ".gitignore" file in your project directory, which list the files to be ignored, as follows:

```
# .gitignore

# Java class files
*.class

# Executable files
*.exe

# Object and archive files
# Can use regular expression, e.g., [oa] matches
either o or a
*.[oa]

# temp sub-directory (ended with a directory
separator)
temp/
```

There should NOT be any trailing comments for filename. You can use regexe for matching the filename/pathname patterns, e.g. [oa] denotes either o or a. You can override the rules by using the inverted pattern (!), e.g., Adding

!hello.exe includes the hello.exe although *.exe are excluded.

Now, issue a "git status" command to check the untracked files.

```
$ git status
On branch master
Untracked files:
  (use "git add <file>..." to include in what will be
committed)
      .gitignore
nothing added to commit but untracked files present
(use "git add" to track)
```

Now, "Hello.class" is not shown in "Untracked files".

Typically, we also track and commit the .gitignore file.

```
$ git add .gitignore

$ git status
On branch master
Changes to be committed:
  (use "git reset HEAD <file>..." to unstage)
        new file:   .gitignore

$ git commit -m "Added .gitignore"
[master 711ef4f] Added .gitignore
 1 file changed, 14 insertions(+)
 create mode 100644 .gitignore

$ git status
On branch master
nothing to commit, working directory clean
```

Setting up Remote Repo

1. Sign up for a GIT host, such as Github https://github.com/signup/free (Unlimited for public projects; fee for private projects); or BitBucket @ https://bitbucket.org/ (Unlimited users for public projects; 5 free users for private projects; Unlimited for Academic Plan); among others.
2. Login to the GIT host. Create a new remote repo called "test".
3. On your local repo (let's continue to work on our "hello-git" project), set up the remote repo's name and URL via "git remote add <remote-name> <remote-url>" command.

By convention, we shall name our remote repo as "origin". You can find the URL of a remote repo from the Git host. The URL may take the form of HTTPS or SSH. Use HTTPS for simplicity.

```
// Change directory to your local repo's working
directory
$ cd /path-to/hello-git

// Add a remote repo called "origin" via "git remote
add <remote-name> <remote-url>"
// For examples,
```

```
$ git remote add origin https://github.com/your-
username/test.git                // for GitHub
$ git remote add origin
https://username@bitbucket.org/your-username/test.git
// for Bitbucket
```

You can list all the remote names and their corresponding URLs via "git remote -v", for example,

```
// List all remote names and their corresonding URLs
$ git remote -v
origin  https://github.com/your-username/test.git
(fetch)
origin  https://github.com/your-username/test.git
(push)
```

Now, you can manage the remote connection, using a simple name instead of the complex URL.

4. Push the commits from the local repo to the remote repo via "git push -u <remote-name> <local-branch-name>".

By convention, the main branch of our local repo is called "master" (as seen from the earlier "git status" output). We shall discuss "branch" later.

```
// Push all commits of the branch "master" to remote
repo "origin"
$ git push origin master
Username for 'https://github.com': ******
Password for 'https://your-username@github.com':
*******
Counting objects: 10, done.
Delta compression using up to 8 threads.
Compressing objects: 100% (10/10), done.
Writing objects: 100% (10/10), 1.13 KiB | 0 bytes/s,
done.
Total 10 (delta 1), reused 0 (delta 0)
To https://github.com/your-username/test.git
 * [new branch]      master -> master
Branch master set up to track remote branch master
from origin.
```

5. Login to the GIT host and select the remote repo "test", you shall find all the committed files.

6. On your local system, make some change (e.g., on "Hello.java"); stage and commit the changes on the local repo; and push it to the remote. This is known as the "Edit/Stage/Commit/Push" cycle.

```
// Hello.java
public class Hello {
   public static void main(String[] args) {
      System.out.println("Hello, world from GIT!");
      System.out.println("Changes after First
commit!");
      System.out.println("Changes after Pushing to
remote!");
   }
}
```

```
$ git status
On branch master
Your branch is up-to-date with 'origin/master'.

Changes not staged for commit:
  (use "git add <file>..." to update what will be
committed)
  (use "git checkout -- <file>..." to discard changes
in working dire
      modified:   Hello.java
no changes added to commit (use "git add" and/or "git
commit -a")

// Stage file changes
$ git add *.java

$ git status
On branch master
Your branch is up-to-date with 'origin/master'.

Changes to be committed:
  (use "git reset HEAD <file>..." to unstage)
        modified:   Hello.java

// Commit all staged file changes
$ git commit -m "Third commit"
[master 744307e] Third commit
 1 file changed, 1 insertion(+)

// Push the commits on local master branch to remote
$ git push origin master
Username for 'https://github.com': ******
Password for 'https://username@github.com': ******
Counting objects: 5, done.
Delta compression using up to 8 threads.
Compressing objects: 100% (3/3), done.
Writing objects: 100% (3/3), 377 bytes | 0 bytes/s,
done.
Total 3 (delta 1), reused 0 (delta 0)
```

```
To https://github.com/your-username/test.git
   711ef4f..744307e  master -> master
```

Again, login to the remote to check the committed files.

CLONING A PROJECT FROM A REMOTE REPO (GIT CLONE <REMOTE-URL>)

As mentioned earlier, you can start a local GIT repo either running "git init" on your own project, or "git clone <remote-url>" to copy from an existing project.

Anyone having read access to your remote repo can clone your project. You can also clone any project in any public remote repo.

The "git clone <remote-url>" initializes a local repo and copies all files into the working tree. You can find the URL of a remote repo from the Git host.

```
// SYNTAX
// ======
$ git clone <remote-url>
   // <url>: can be https (recommended), ssh or file.
   // Clone the project UNDER the current directory
   // The name of the "working directory" is the same
as the remote project name
$ git clone <remote-url> <working-directory-name>
   // Clone UNDER current directory, use the given
"working directory" name

// EXAMPLES
// ========
// Change directory (cd) to the "parent" directory of
the project directory
$ cd path-to-parent-of-the-working-directory
```

```
// Clone our remote repo "test" into a new working
directory called "hello-git-cloned"
$ git clone https://github.com/your-username/test.git
hello-git-cloned
Cloning into 'hello-git-cloned'...
remote: Counting objects: 13, done.
remote: Compressing objects: 100% (11/11), done.
remote: Total 13 (delta 2), reused 13 (delta 2)
Unpacking objects: 100% (13/13), done.
Checking connectivity... done.

// Verify
$ cd hello-git-cloned

$ ls -a
.  ..  .git  .gitignore  Hello.java  README.md

$ git status
On branch master
Your branch is up-to-date with 'origin/master'.
nothing to commit, working directory clean
```

The "git clone" automatically creates a remote name called "origin" mapped to the cloned remote-URL. You can check via "git remote -v":

```
// List all the remote names
$ git remote -v
origin  https://github.com/your-username/test.git
(fetch)
origin  https://github.com/your-username/test.git
(push)
```

Summary of Basic "Edit/Stage/Commit/Push" Cycle

```
// Edit (Create, Modified, Rename, Delete) files,
//  which produces "unstaged" file changes.

// Stage file changes, which produces "Staged" file
changes
$ git add <file>                           // for new
and modified files
$ git rm <file>                            // for
deleted files
$ git mv <old-file-name> <new-file-name>  // for
renamed file

// Commit (ALL staged file changes)
$ git commit -m "message"

// Push
$ git push <remote-name> <local-branch-name>
```

OR,

```
// Stage ALL files with changes
$ git add -A   // OR, 'git add --all'

$ git commit -m "message"
$ git push
```

OR,

```
// Add All and Commit in one command
$ git commit -a -m "message"
```

```
$ git push
```

More on Staged and Unstaged Changes

If you modify a file, stage the changes and modify the file again, there will be staged changes and unstaged changes for that file.

For example, let's continue the "hello-git" project. Add one more line to "README.md" and stage the changes:

```
// README.md
This is the README file for the Hello-world project.
Make some changes and staged.


$ git status
On branch master
Your branch is up-to-date with 'origin/master'.
Changes not staged for commit:
        modified:   README.md

$ git add README.md

$ git status
On branch master
Your branch is up-to-date with 'origin/master'.
Changes to be committed:
        modified:   README.md
```

Before the changes are committed, suppose we modify the file again:

```
// README.md
This is the README file for the Hello-world project.
Make some changes and staged.
Make more changes before the previous changes are
committed.


$ git status
On branch master
Your branch is up-to-date with 'origin/master'.

Changes to be committed:
        modified:   README.md

Changes not staged for commit:
        modified:   README.md

// Now, "README.md" has both unstaged and staged
changes.

// Show the staged changes
$ git diff --staged
diff --git a/README.md b/README.md
index 9565113..b2e9afb 100644
--- a/README.md
+++ b/README.md
@@ -1,2 +1,3 @@
 // README.md
 This is the README file for the Hello-world project.
+Make some changes and staged.

// Show the unstaged changes
$ git diff
diff --git a/README.md b/README.md
index b2e9afb..ca6622a 100644
--- a/README.md
+++ b/README.md
```

```
@@ -1,3 +1,4 @@
 // README.md
 This is the README file for the Hello-world project.
 Make some changes and staged.
+Make more changes before the previous changes are
committed.

// Stage the changes
$ git add README.md

$ git status
On branch master
Your branch is up-to-date with 'origin/master'.

Changes to be committed:
        modified:   README.md

// Show staged changes
$ git diff --staged
diff --git a/README.md b/README.md
index 9565113..ca6622a 100644
--- a/README.md
+++ b/README.md
@@ -1,2 +1,4 @@
 // README.md
 This is the README file for the Hello-world project.
+Make some changes and staged.
+Make more changes before the previous changes are
committed.

// Commit the staged changes
$ git commit -m "Unstaged vs. Staged Changes"
[master a44199b] Unstaged vs. Staged Changes
 1 file changed, 2 insertions(+), 0 deletion(-)
```

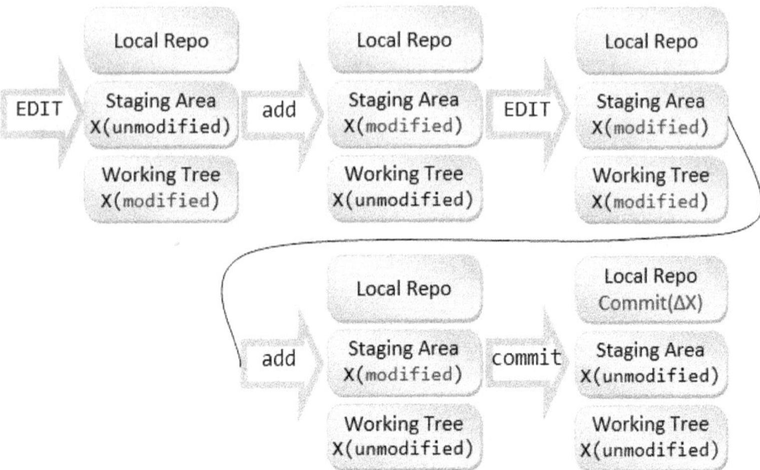

Take note that the stage changes are cleared when the changes are committed; while the unstaged changes are cleared when the changes are staged.

For convenience, you can also use the "git-gui" tool to view the unstaged and staged changes.

GIT GUI TOOLS

GIT-GUI (WINDOWS)

For convenience, Git provides a GUI tool, called git-gui, which can be used to perform all tasks and view the commit log graphically.

Install "Git-Gui".

To run the git-gui, you can right-click on the project folder and choose "Git Gui"; or launch the Git-bash shell and run "git gui" command.

To view the log, choose "Repository" ⇒ "Visualize master's history", which launches the "gitk". You can view the details of each commit.

You can also view each of the file via "Repository" ⇒ "Browse master's Files" ⇒ Select a file.

Git-gui is bundled with Git. To launch git-gui, right click on the working directory and choose "git gui", or run "git gui" command on the Git-Bash shell.

TAGGING

Tag (or label) can be used to tag a specific commit as being important, for example, to mark a particular release. The release is often marked in this format: version-number.release-no.modificaton-no (e.g., v1.1.5) or or version-number.release-no.upgrade-no_modificaton-no (e.g., v1.7.0_26).

I recommend that you commit your code and push it to the remote repo as often as needed (e.g., daily), to BACKUP your code. When you code reaches a stable point (in turn of functionality), create a tag to mark the commit, which can then be used for CHECKOUT, if you need to show your code to others.

LISTING TAGS (GIT TAG)

To list the existing tags, use "git tag" command.

Types of Tags - Lightweight Tags and Annotated Tags

There are two kinds of tags: lightweight tag and annotated tag. Lightweight tag is simply a pointer to a commit. Annotated tag contains annotations (meta-data) and can be digitally signed and verified.

Creating an Annotated Tag (git tag -a <tag-name> -m <message>)

To create an annotated tag at the latest commit, use "git tag -a <tag-name> -m <message>", where -a option specifies annotation tag having meta-data. For example,

$ git tag -a v1.0.0 -m "First production system"

```
// List all tags
$ git tag
v1.0.0

// Show tag details
$ git show v1.0.0
   // Show the commit point and working tree
```

To create a tag for an earlier commit, you need to find out the commit's name (first seven character hash code) (via "git log"), and issue "git tag -a <tag-name> -m <message> <commit-name>". For example,

```
$ git log
......
commit 7e7cb40a9340691e2b16a041f7185cee5f7ba92e
......
    Commit 3

$ git tag -a "v0.9.0" -m "Last pre-production
release" 7e7cb40

// List all tags
$ git tag
v0.9.0
v1.0.0

// Show details of a tag
$ git show v0.9.0
```

Creating Lightweight Tags (git tag <tag-name>)

To create a lightweight tag (without meta-data), use "git tag <tag-name>" without the -a option. The lightweight tag stores only the commit hash code.

Signed Tags

You can signed your tags with your private key, with -s option instead of -a.

To verify a signed tag, use -v option and provide the signer's public key.

Pushing to Remote Repo

By default, Git does not push tags (and branches) to remote repo. You need to push them explicitly, via "git push origin <tag-name>" for a particular tag or "git push origin --tags" for all the tags.

Branching/Merging

Git's Data Structures

Git has two primary data structures:

1. an immutable, append-only object database (or local repo) that stores all the commits and file contents;
2. a mutable staging area (or index, or cache) that caches the staged information.

The staging area serves as the connection between object database and working tree (as shown in the storage model diagram). It serves to avoid volatility, and allows you to stage ALL the file changes before issuing a commit, instead of committing individual file change. Changes to files that have been explicitly added to the index (staging area) via "git add <file>" are called staged changes. Changes that have not been added are called unstaged changes. Staged and unstaged changes can co-exist. Performing a commit copies the statged changes into object database (local repo) and clears the index. The unstaged changes remain in working tree.

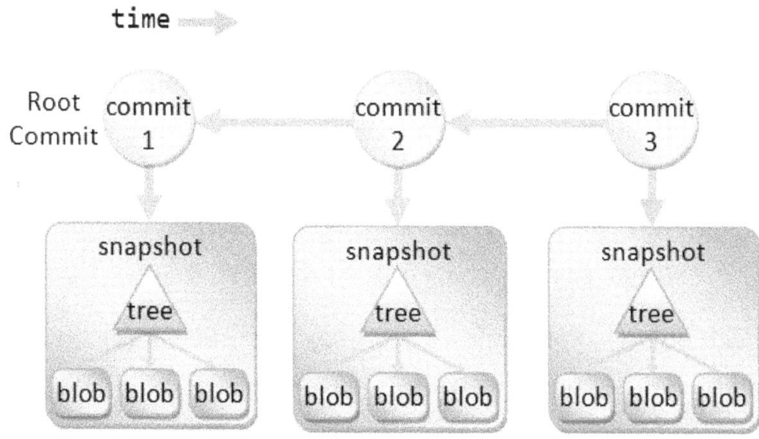

The object database contains these objects:

- Each version of a file is represented by a blob (binary large object - a file that can contain any data: binaries or characters). A blob holds the file data only, without any metadata - not even the filename.
- A snapshot of the working tree is represented by a tree object, which links the blobs and sub-trees for sub-directories.
- A commit object points to a tree object, i.e., the snapshot of the working tree at the point the commit was created. It holds metadata such as timestamp,

log message, author's and committer's username and email. It also references its parent commit(s), except the root commit which has no parent. A normal commit has one parent; a merge commit could have multiple parents. A commit, where new branch is created, has more than one children. By referencing through the chain of parent commit(s), you can discover the history of the project.

Each object is identified (or named) by a 160-bit (or 40 hex-digit) SHA-1 hash value of its contents (i.e., a content-addressable name). Any tiny change to the contents produces a different hash value, resulted in a different object. Typically, we use the first 7 hex-digit prefix to refer to an object, as long as there is no ambiguity.

There are two ways to refer to a particular commit: via a branch or a tag.

- A branch is a mobile reference of commit. It moves forward whenever commit is made on that branch.
- A tag (like a label) marks a particular commit. Tag is often used for marking the releases.

BRANCHING

Branching allows you and your team members to work on different aspects of the software concurrently (on so-called feature branches), and merge into the master branch as and when they completes. Branching is the most important feature in a concurrent version control system.

A branch in Git is a lightweight movable pointer to one of the commits. For the initial commit, Git assigns the default branch name called master and sets the master branch pointer at the initial commit. As you make further commits on the master branch, the master branch pointer move forward accordingly. Git also uses a special pointer called HEAD to keep track of the branch that you are currently working on. The HEAD always refers to the latest commit on the current branch. Whenever you switch branch, the HEAD also switches to the latest commit on the branch switched.

Example

For example, let's create a Git-managed project called git_branch_test with only the a single-line README.md file:

```
This is the README. My email is xxx@somewhere.com
$ git init
$ git add README.md
$ git commit -m "Commit 1"

// Append a line in README.md: This line is added
after Commit 1
$ git status
$ git add README.md
$ git commit -m "Commit 2"

// Append a line in README.md: This line is added
after Commit 2
$ git status
$ git add README.md
$ git commit -m "Commit 3"

// Show all the commits (oneline each)
$ git log --oneline
44fdf4c Commit 3
51f6827 Commit 2
fbed70e Commit 1
```

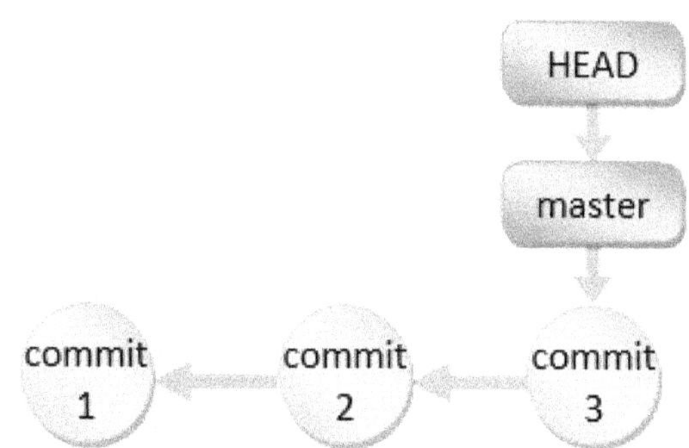

Creating a new Branch (git branch <branch-name>)

You can create a new branch via "git branch <branch-name>" command. When you create a new branch (says devel, or development), Git creates a new branch pointer for the branch devel, pointing initially at the latest commit on the current branch master.

```
$ git branch devel
```

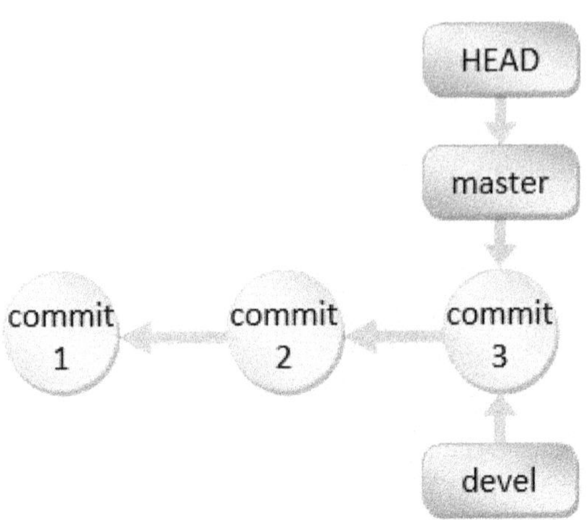

Take note that when you create a new branch, the HEAD pointer is still pointing at the current branch.

Branch Names Convention

- master branch: the production branch with tags for the various releases.
- development (or next or devel) branch: developmental branch, to be merged into master if and when completes.
- topics branch: a short-live branch for a specific topics, such as introducing a feature (for the devel branch) or fixing a bug (for the master branch).

SWITCHING TO A BRANCH (GIT CHECKOUT <BRANCH-NAME>)

Git uses a special pointer called HEAD to keep track of the branch that you are working on. The "git branch <branch-name>" command simply create a branch, but does not switch to the new branch. To switch to a branch, use "git checkout <branch-name>" command. The HEAD pointer will be pointing at the switched branch (e.g., devel).

```
$ git checkout devel
Switched to branch 'devel'
```

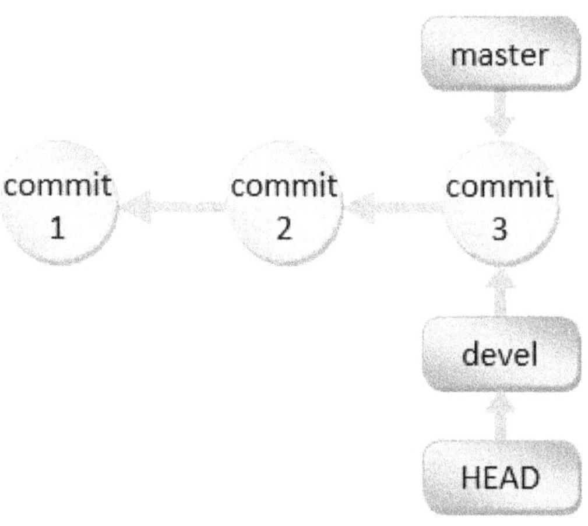

Alternatively, you can use "git checkout -b <branch-name>" to create a new branch and switch into the new branch.

If you switch to a branch and make changes and commit. The HEAD pointer moves forward in that branch.

```
// Append a line in README.md: This line is added on
devel branch after Commit 3
$ git status   // NOTE "On branch devel"
$ git add README.md
$ git commit -m "Commit 4"
[devel c9b88d9] Commit 4
```

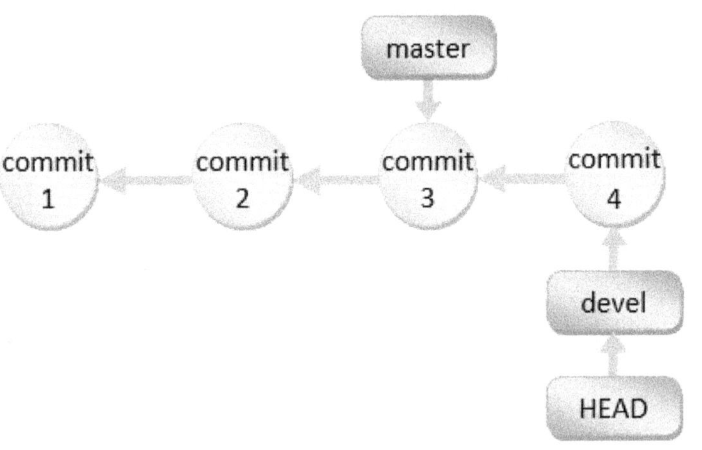

You can switch back to the master branch via "git checkout master". The HEAD pointer moves back to the last commit of the master branch, and the working directory is rewinded back to the latest commit on the master branch.

```
$ git checkout master
Switched to branch 'master'
// Check the content of the README.md, which is
reminded back to Commit 3
```

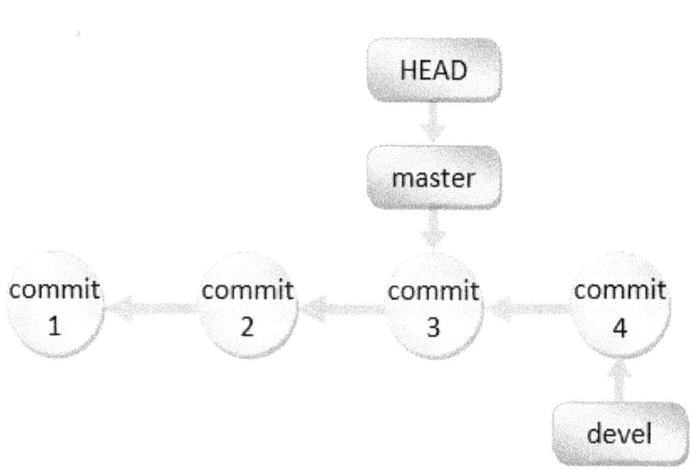

If you continue to work on the master branch and commit, the HEAD pointer moves forward on the master branch. The two branches now diverge.

```
// Append a line in README.md: This line is added on
master branch after Commit 4
$ git status    // NOTE "On branch master"
$ git add README.md
$ git commit -m "Commit 5"
[master 6464eb8] Commit 5
```

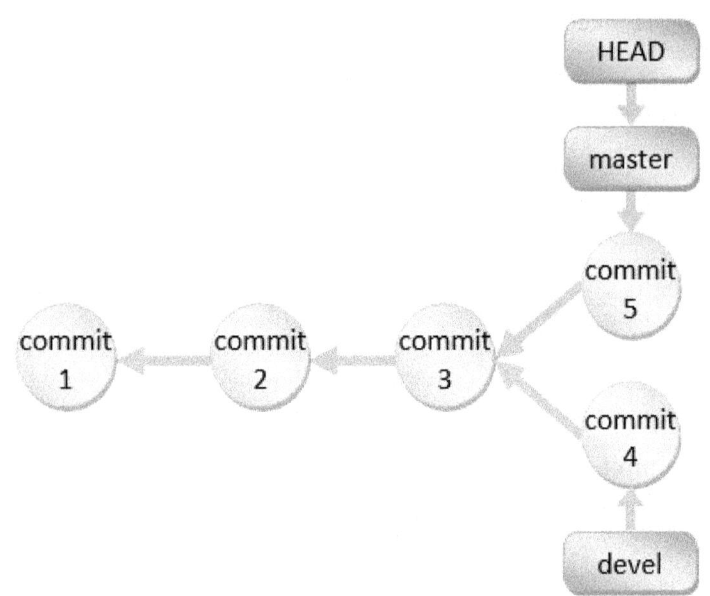

If you check out the devel branch, the file contents will be rewinded back to Commit-4.

```
$ git checkout devel
// Check file contents
```

MERGING TWO BRANCHES (GIT MERGE <BRANCH-NAME>)

To merge two branches, says master and devel, check out the first branch, e,g, master, (via "git checkout <branch-name>") and merge with another branch, e.g., devel, via command "git merge <branch-name>".

FAST-FORWARD LINEAR MERGE

If the branch to be merged is a direct descendant, Git performs fast forward by moving the HEAD pointer forward. For example, suppose that you are currently working on the devel branch at commit-4, and the master branch's latest commit is at commit-3:

```
$ git checkout master

// Let discard the Commit-5 totally and rewind to
commit-3 on master branch
// This is solely for illustration!!! Do this with
great care!!!
$ git reset --hard HEAD~1
HEAD is now at 7e7cb40 Commit 3
  // HEAD~1 moves the HEAD pointer back by one commit
(-1)
  // --hard also resets the working tree
```

```
// Check the file contents

$ git merge devel
Updating 7e7cb40..4848c7b
Fast-forward
 README.md | 1 +
 1 file changed, 1 insertion(+)

// Check the file contents
```

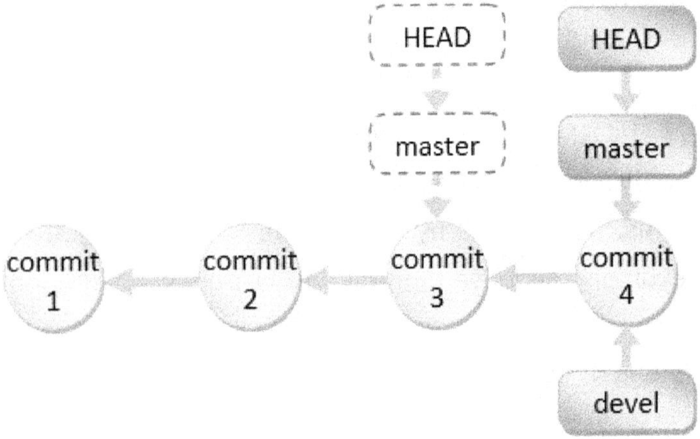

Take note that no new commit is created.

3-WAY MERGE

If the two branches are diverged, git automatically searches for the common ancestor commit and performs a 3-way merge. If there is no conflict, a new commit will be created.

If git detects a conflict, it will pause the merge and issue a merge conflict and ask you to resolve the conflict manually. The file is marked as unmerged. You can issue "git status" to check the unmerged files, study the details of the conflict, and decide which way to resolve the conflict. Once the conflict is resolve, stage the file (via "git add <file>"). Finally, run a "git commit" to finalize the 3-way merge (the same Edit/Stage/Commit cycle).

```
$ git checkout master
// undo the Commit-4, back to Commit-3
$ git reset --hard HEAD~1
HEAD is now at 7e7cb40 Commit 3

// Change the email to abc@abc.com
$ git add README.md
$ git commit -m "Commit 5"

$ git checkout devel
// undo the Commit-4, back to Commit-3
$ git reset --hard HEAD~1
// Change the email to xyz@xyz.com to trigger
conflict
$ git add README.md
$ git commit -m "Commit 4"
```

```
// Let's do a 3-way merge with conflict
$ git checkout master
$ git merge devel
Auto-merging README.md
CONFLICT (content): Merge conflict in README.md
Automatic merge failed; fix conflicts and then commit
the result.

$ git status
# On branch master
# You have unmerged paths.
#   (fix conflicts and run "git commit")
#
# Unmerged paths:
#   (use "git add <file>..." to mark resolution)
#       both modified:      README.md
no changes added to commit (use "git add" and/or "git
commit -a")
```

The conflict file is marked as follows (in "git status"):

```
<<<<<<< HEAD
This is the README. My email is abc@abc.com
=======
This is the README. My email is xyz@xyz.com
>>>>>>> devel
This line is added after Commit 1
This line is added after Commit 2
```

You need to manually decide which way to take, or you could discard both by setting the email to zzz@nowhere.com.

```
$ git add README.md
$ git commit -m "Commit 6"
```

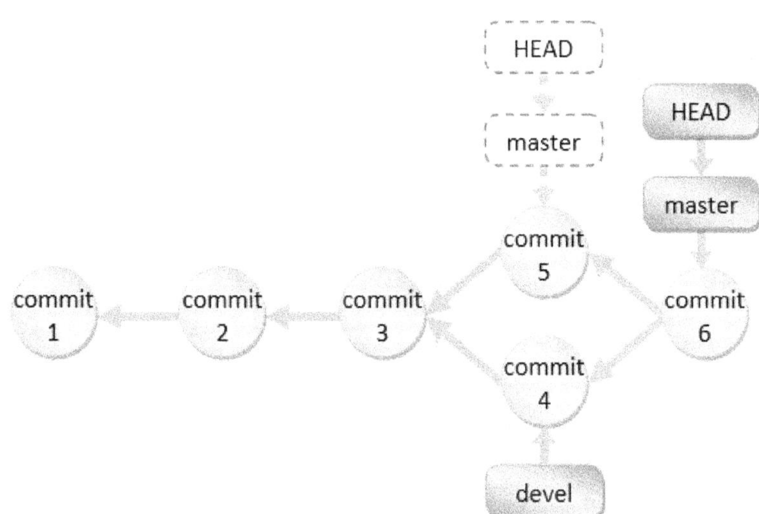

Take note that In a 3-way merge, a new commit will be created in the process (unlike fast-forward merge).

DELETING A MERGED BRANCH (GIT BRANCH -D <BRANCH-NAME>)

The merged branch (e.g., devel) is no longer needed. You can delete it via "git branch -d <branch-name>".

```
$ git branch -d devel
Deleted branch devel (was a20f002).

// Create the development branch again at the latest
commit
$ git branch devel
```

REBASING BRANCH (GIT REBASE)

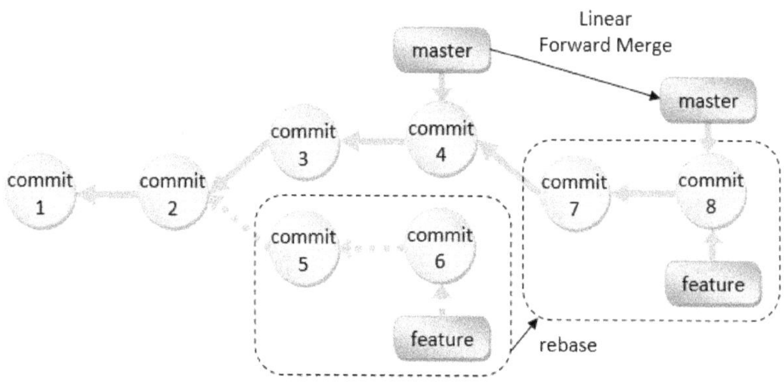

The primary purpose for rebasing is to maintain a linear project history. For example, if you checkout a devel branch and work on commit-5 and commit-6, instead of doing a 3-way merge into the master branch and subsequently remove the devel branch, you can rebase the commit-5 and commit-6, on commit-4, and perform a linear forward merge to maintain all the project history. New commits (7 and 8) will be created for the rebased commit (5 and 6).

The syntax is:

```
// SYNTAX
$ git rebase <base-name>
   // <base-name> could be any kind of commit
reference
   // (such as an commit-name, a branch name, a tag,
   // or a relative reference to HEAD).
```

Examples:

```
// Start a new feature branch from the current master
$ git checkout -b feature master
// Edit/Stage/Commit changes to feature branch

// Need to work on a fix on the master
$ git checkout -b hotfix master
// Edit/Stage/Commit changes to hotfix branch
// Merge hotfix into master
$ git checkout master
$ git merge hotfix
// Delete hotfix branch
$ git branch -d hotfix

// Rebase feature branch on master branch
//  to maintain a linear history
$ git checkout feature
$ git rebase master
// Now, linear merge
$ git checkout master
$ git merge feature
```

Amend the Last Commit (git commit --amend)

If you make a commit but want to change the commit message or adding more changes, you may amend the recent commit (instead of creating new commit) via command "git commit --amend"):

```
$ git commit --amend -m "message"
```

For example,

```
// Do a commit
$ git commit -m "added login menu"

// Realize that you have not staged some files.
// Amend the commit
$ git add morefile
$ git commit --amend
    // You could modify the commit message here
```

More on "git checkout" and Detached HEAD

"git checkout" can be used to checkout a branch, a commit, or files. The syntaxes are:

```
$ git checkout <branch-name>
$ git checkout <commit-name>
$ git checkout <commit-name> <filename>
```

When you checkout a commit, Git switches into so-called "Detached HEAD" state, i.e., the HEAD detached from the tip of a branch. Suppose that you continue to work on the detached HEAD on commit-5, and wish to merge the commit-5 back to master. You checkout the master branch, but there is no branch name for your to reference the commit-5!!!

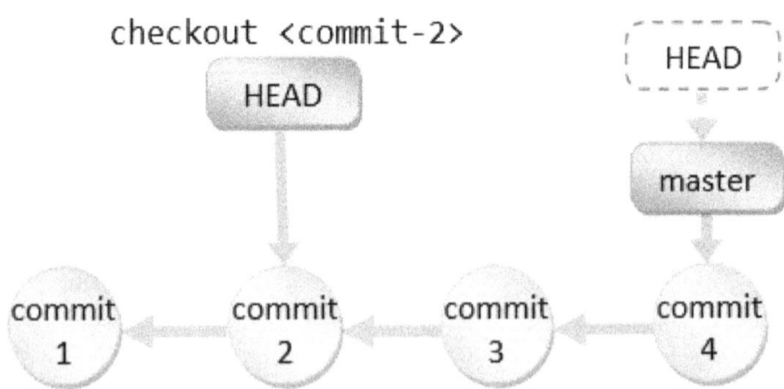

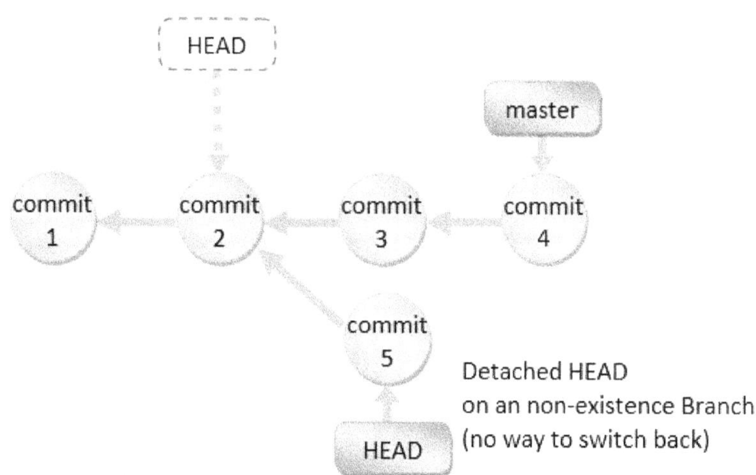

In Summary, you can use "git checkout <commit-name>" to inspect a commit. BUT you should always work on a branch, NOT on a detached HEAD.

More on "git reset" and "git reset --hard"

```
$ git reset <file>
   // Unstage the changes of <file> from staging
area,
   //   not affecting the working tree.

$ git reset
   // Reset the staging area
   // Remove all changes (of all files) from staging
area,
   //   not affecting the working tree.

$ git reset --hard
   // Reset the staging area and working tree to
match the
   //   recent commit  (i.e., discard all changes
since the
   //   last commit).

$ git reset <commit-name>
   // Move the HEAD of current branch to the given
commit,
   //   not affecting the working tree.

$ git reset --hard <commit-name>
   // Reset both staging area and working tree to the
given
   //   commit, i.e., discard all changes after that
commit.
```

GIT REVERT <COMMIT-NAME>

The "git revert" undoes a commit. But, instead of removing the commit from the project history, it undos the changes introduced by the commit and appends a new commit with the resulting content. This prevents Git from losing history. "git revert" is a safer way comparing with "git reset".

```
// SYNTAX
$ git revert <commit-name>

// EXAMPLE
[TODO] example and diagram
```

SUMMARY OF WORK FLOWS

SETTING UP GIT AND "EDIT/STAGE/COMMIT/PUSH" CYCLE

Step 1: Install GIT.

- For Windows and Mac, download the installer from http://git-scm.com/downloads and run the downloaded installer.
- For Ubuntu, issue command "sudo apt-get install git".

For Windows, use "git-bash" command shell provided by Windows installer to issue command. For Mac/Ubuntu, use "Terminal".

Step 2: Configuring GIT:

```
// Setup your username and email to be used in
labeling commits
$ git config --global user.email "your-
email@yourmail.com"
$ git config --global user.name "your-name"
Step 3: Set up GIT repo for a project. For example,
we have a project called "olas1.1" located at
"/usr/local/olas/olas1.1".

$ cd /usr/local/olas/olas1.1
 // Initialize the GIT repo
$ git init

$ ls -al
```

```
// Check for ".git" directory
```

Create a "README.md" (or "README.textile" if you are using Eclipse's WikiText in "textile" markup) under your project directory to describe the project.

Step 4: Start "Edit/Stage/Commit/Push" cycles.

Create/Modify files. Stage files into the staging area via "git add <file>".

```
// Check the status
$ git status
......

// Add files into repo
$ git add README.md
$ git add www
......

// Check the status
$ git status
```

Step 5: Create a ".gitignore" (in the project base directory) to exclude folders/files from being tracked by GIT. Check your "git status" output to decide which folders/files to be ignored.

For example,

```
# ignore files and directories beginning with dot
.*

# ignore directories beginning with dot (a directory
ends with a slash)
.*/

# ignore these files and directories
www/test/
www/.*
www/.*/
The trailing slash indicate directory (and its sub-
directories and files).

If you want the ".gitignore" to be tracked (which is
in the ignore list):

$ git add -f .gitignore
      // -f to override the .gitignore
```

Step 6: Commit.

```
$ git status
......

// Commit with a message
$ git commit -m "Initial Commit"
......

$ git status
```

Step 7: Push to the Remote Repo (for backup, version control, and collaboration).

You need to first crea te a repo (says olas) in a remote GIT host, such as GitHub or BitBucket. Take note of the remote repo URL, e.g., https://username@hostname.org/username/olas.git.

```
$ cd /path-to/local-repo

// Add a remote repo name called "origin" mapped to
the remote URL
$ git remote add origin
https://hostname/username/olas.git

// Push the "master" branch to the remote "origin"
// "master" is the default branch name of your local
repo after init.
$ git push origin master
```

Check the remote repo for the files committed.

Step 8: Work on the source files, make changes, commit and push to remote repo.

```
// Check the files modified
$ git status
......

// Stage for commit the modified files
```

```
$ git add ....
......

// Commit (with a message)
$ git commit -m "commit-message"

// Push to remote repo
$ git push origin master
```

Step 9: Create a "tag" (for version number).

```
// Tag a version number to the current commit
$ git tag -a v1.1 -m "Version 1.1"
      // -a to create an annotated tag, -m to provide
a message

// Display all tags
$ git tag
......

// Push the tags to remote repo
// ("git push -u origin master" does not push the
tags)
$ git push origin -tags
```

BRANCH AND MERGE WORKFLOW

It is a good practice to freeze the "master" branch for production; and work on a development branch (says "devel") instead. You may often spawn a branch to fix a bug in the production.

```
// Create a branch called "devel" and checkout.
// The "devel" is initially synchronized with the
"master" branch.
$ git checkout -b devel
      // same as:
      // $ git branch devel
      // $ git checkout

// Edit/Stage/Commit
$ git add <file>
$ git commit -m "commit-message"

// To merge the "devel" into the production "master"
branch
$ git checkout master
$ git merge devel

// Push both branches to remote repo
$ git push origin master devel

// Checkout the "devel" branch and continue...
$ git checkout devel
   // Edit/Stage/Commit/Push

// Need to fix a bug in production (in "master"
branch)
$ git checkout master
```

```
// Spawn a "fix" branch to fix the bug, and merge
with the "master" branch

// To remove the "devel" branch (if the branch is
out-of-sync)
$ git branch -d devel
// To re-create the "devel" branch
$ git checkout -b devel
```

VIEWING THE COMMIT GRAPH (GITK)

You can use the "git-gui" "gitk" tool to view the commit graph.

To run the git-gui, you can right-click on the project folder and choose "Git Gui"; or launch the Git-bash shell and run "git gui" command.

To view the commit graph, choose "Repository" ⇒ "Visualize master's history", which launches the "gitk". You can view the details of each commit.

Synchronizing Remote and Local: Fetch/Merge, Pull and Push

Setup up a remote repo (revision)

As described earlier, you can use "git remote" command to set up a "remote name", mapped to the URL of a remote repo.

```
// Add a new "remote name" maps to the URL of a
remote repo
$ git remote add <remote-name> <remote-url>
// For example,
$ git remote add origin
https://hostname/username/project-name.git
    // Define a new remote name "origin" mapping to
the given URL

// List all the remote names
$ git remote -v

// Delete a remote name
$ git remote rm <remote-name>

// Rename a remote name
$ git remote rename <old-remote-name> <new-remote-
name>
```

Cloning a Remote Repo (revision)

```
$ git clone <remote-url>
```

```
    // Init a GIT local repo and copy all objects
from the remote repo
$ git clone <remote-url> <working-directory-name>
   // Use the working-directory-name instead of
default to project name
```

Whenever you clone a remote repo using command "git clone <remote-url>", a remote name called "origin" is automatically added and mapped to <remote-url>.

Fetch/Merge Changes from remote (git fetch/merge)

The "git fetch" command imports commits from a remote repo to your local repo, without updating your local working tree. This gives you a chance to review changes before updating (merging into) your working tree. The fetched objects are stored in remote branches, that are differentiated from the local branches.

```
$ cd /path-to/working-directory

$ git fetch <remote-name>
   // Fetch ALL branches from the remote repo to your
local repo

$ git fetch <remote-name> <branch-name>
   // Fetch the specific branch from the remote repo
to your local repo

// List the local branches
```

```
$ git branch
* master
  devel
   // * indicates current branch

// List the remote branches
$ git branch -r
  origin/master
  origin/devel

// You can checkout a remote branch to inspect the
files/commits.
// But this put you into "Detached HEAD" state, which
prevent you
// from updating the remote branch.

// You can merge the fetched changes into local repo
$ git checkout master
   // Switch to "master" branch of local repo
$ git merge origin/master
   // Merge the fetched changes from stored remote
branch to local
```

GIT PULL

As a short hand, "git pull" combines "git fetch" and "git merge" into one command, for convenience.

```
$ git pull <remote-name>
   // Fetch the remote's copy of the current branch
and merge it
   //  into the local repo immediately, i.e., update
the working tree

// Same as
$ git fetch <remote-name> <current-branch-name>
$ git merge <remote-name> <current-branch-name>
```

```
$ git pull --rebase <remote-name>
   // linearize local changes after the remote
branch.
```

The "git pull" is an easy way to synchronize your local repo with origin's (or upstream) changes (for a specific branch).

Pushing to Remote Repo (Revision)

The "git push <remote-name> <branch-name>" is the counterpart of "git fetch", which exports commits from local repo to remote repo.

```
$ git push <remote-name> <branch-name>
   // Push the specific branch of the local repo

$ git push <remote-name> --all
   // Push all branches of the local repo

$ git push <remote-name> --tag
   // Push all tags
   // "git push" does not push tags

$ git push -u <remote-name> <branch-name>
   // Save the remote-name and branch-name as the
   // reference (or current) remote-name and branch-
name.
   // Subsequent "git push" without argument will use
these references.
```

"Fork" and "Pull Request"

"Fork" and "Pull Request" are features provided by GIT hosts (such as GitHub and BitBucket):

- Pushing "Fork" button to copy a project from an account (e.g., project maintainer) to your own personal account. [TODO] diagram
- Pushing "Pull Request" button to notify other developers (e.g., project maintainer or the entire project team) to review your changes. If accepted, the project maintainer can pull and apply the changes. A pull request shall provide the source's repo name, source's branch name, destination's repo name and destination's branch name.

Feature-Branch Workflow for Shared Repo

Feature-Branch workflow is more prevalent with small teams on private projects. Everyone in the team is granted push access to a single shared remote repository and feature (or topic) branches are used to isolate changes made by the team members.

The project maintainer starts the "master" branch on the shared remote repo. All developers clone the "master" branch into their local repos. Each developer starts a feature branch (e.g., "user1-featureX") to work on a feature. Once completed (or even work-in-progress), he files a "pull request" to initiate a review for his feature. All developers can provide comments and suggestions. Once accepted, the project maintainer can then merge the feature branch into the "master" branch.

1) setup

Remote Repo
origin/master
origin/carol-feature

4) File "pull request"

2) clone
(origin/master
-> master)

3a) branch
(carol-feature)

3b) add/commit
(carol-feature)

3c) push
(carol-feature
-> origin/carol-feature)

Carol's Local Repo
master
carol-feature

Changes accepted by Mark

Remote Repo
origin/master
origin/carol-feature

7b) pull
(origin/master
-> master)

7c) pull
(origin/carol-feature
-> master)

7a) checkout
(master)

7d) push
(master
-> origin/master)

Mark's Local Repo
master

The steps are:

1. Mark, the project maintainer, starts the project by pushing to the shared remote repo's "master" branch.
2. Carol, a contributor, clones the project into her local repo, via:

   ```
   // Carol:
   $ cd parent-directory-of-the-working-directory
   $ git clone https://hostname/path-to/project-name.git
       // Create a remote-name "origin" (default), 
   branch "master"
       //  on her local repo
   ```

3. Carol starts a feature branch (says "carol-feature") under the "master" branch to work on a new feature, via:

   ```
   // Carol:
   $ git checkout -b carol-feature master
      // Create a new branch "carol-feature" under 
   "master" branch
      //   and switch to the new branch

   // Edit/Stage/Commit/Push cycles on carol-feature 
   branch
   $ git status
   $ git add <file>
   $ git commit -m <message>
   $ git push origin carol-feature

   // Repeat until done
   ```

4. Carol completes the new feature. She files a "pull request" (by pushing the "pull request" button on the Git host) to notify the rest of the team members.

5. Mark, the project maintainer, or anyone in the team, can comment on Carol's feature. Carol can re-work on the feature, if necessary, and pushes all subsequent commits under her feature branch.

6. Once the feature is accepted, Mark, or anyone in the team (including Carol), performs a merge to apply the feature branch into the "master" branch:

```
// Mark, or Anyone:
$ git checkout master
   // Switch to the "master" branch of the local repo
$ git pull origin master
   // Fetch and merge the latest changes on local's
"master" branch,
   //   if any (i.e., synchronize)
$ git pull origin carol-feature
   // Fetch and merge carol-feature branch on local's
"master" branch
$ git push origin master
   // Update the shared remote repo
```

7. Everyone can update their local repo, via:

```
// Everyone:
$ git checkout master
   // Switch to the "master" branch of the local repo
$ git pull origin master
   // Fetch and merge the latest changes on local
"master" branch
```

FORKING WORKFLOW

In Forking workflow, Instead of using a common shared remote repo, each developer forks the project to his own personal account on the re mote host. He then works on his feature (preferably in a feature branch). Once completed, he files a "pull request" to notify the maintainer to review his changes, and if accepted, merge the changes.

Forking workflow is applicable to developers working in small teams and to a third-party developer contributing to an open source project.

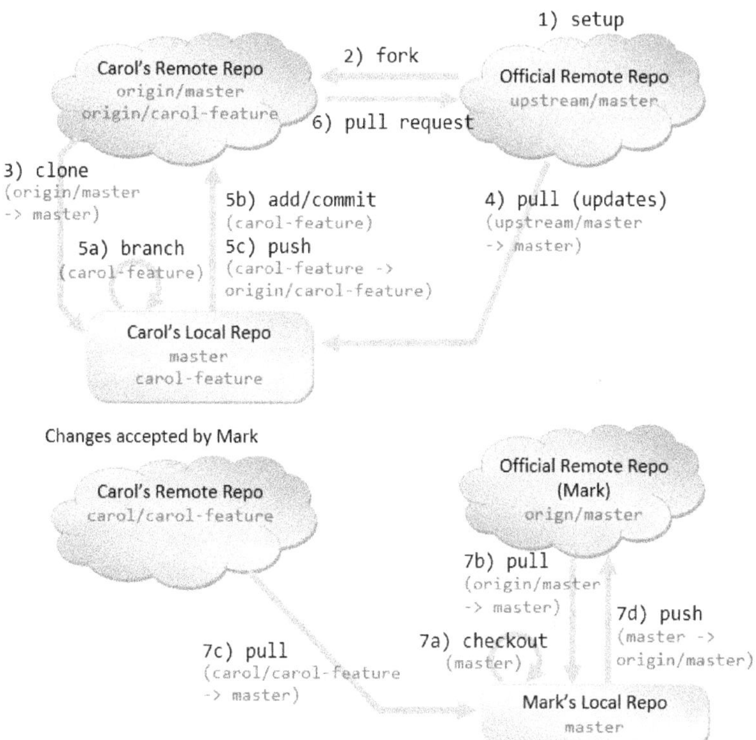

The steps are:

1. Mark, the project maintainer, pushes the project from his local repo ("master" branch) to a remote Git host. He permits "read" access by contributors.

2. Carol, a contributor, gotos Mark's repo, forks the project (by pushing the fork button). "Forking" copies the project to Carol's own personal account on the same Git host.

3. Carol then clones the project from her forked repo into her local repo, via:

```
// Carol:
$ cd parent-directory-of-the-working-directory
$ git clone https://hostname/carol/project-name.git
   // Create a remote name "origin" automatically
   // Copy the "master" branch
```

4. When a fork is cloned, Git creates a remote-name called origin that points to the fork, not the original repo it was forked from. To keep track of the original repo, Carol creates a remote name called "upstream" and pulls (fetches and merges) all new changes:

```
// Carol:
$ cd carol-local-repo-of-the-fork
$ git remote add upstream
https://hostname/mark/project-name.git
   // Create a remote-name "upstream" pointing to the
original remote repo

$ git remote -v
   // List all the remote names and URLs
   // origin: mapped to Carol's forked remote repo
```

```
   // upstream: mapped to Mark's original remote repo

$ git pull upstream master
   // Fetch and merge all changes from the original
remote repo to local repo
   //   for the "master" branch
```

5. Now, Carol can make changes on her local repo (on a new branch), stage and commit the changes, and pushes them to her forked remote repo (so called Edit/Stage/Commit/Push cycles):

```
// Carol:
$ git checkout -b carol-feature master
   // Create a new branch called "carol-feature"
under "master"
   //  and switch to the new branch

// Edit/Stage/Commit/Push cycles on "carol-feature"
branch
$ git status
$ git add <file>
$ git commit -m <message>
$ git push origin carol-feature

// Repeat until done
```

6. Carol files a pull request to Mark (the project maintainer) by pushing the pull-request button. She needs to specify her forked remote repo-name, her branch name (carol-

feature), Mark's remote repo-name, and Mark's branch name (master).

7. Mark opens the pull request (in pull request tab), reviews the change, and decides whether to accept the changes. Mark can ask Carol to re-work on the feature. Carol repeats the Edit/Stage/Commit/Push cycles.

   If Mark decides to accept the changes, he pushes the "Merge" button to merge Carol's contribution to his master branch on the remote repo.

   [If there is no "Merge" button] Mark needs to do the following:

```
// Mark:
$ git checkout master
   // Checkout the "master" branch of the local repo

$ git remote add carol git://hostname/carol/project-
name.git
   // Add a new remote pointing to the Carol's forked
remote repo

$ git pull carol carol-feature
   // Fetch and merge the changes into local repo's
master branch

$ git push origin master
   // Push the update to the Mark's original remote
repo
```

8. All contributors (including Mark and Carol) shall regularly synchronize their local repo by fetch/merge with Mark's master branch.

```
// Carol (and everyone):
$ git checkout master
   // Switch to the "master" branch of the local repo
$ git pull upstream master
   // Fetch and merge the latest changes on "master"
branch from
   //  original remote repo to his local repo
```

OTHER WORKFLOWS

There are other workflows such as "Centralized Workflow" and "GitFlow Workflow". Read "https://www.atlassian.com/git/tutorials/comparing-workflows/gitflow-workflow".

MISCELLANEOUS AND HOW-TO

STAGE AND COMMIT (GIT COMMIT -A -M <MESSAGE>)

You can skip the staging (i.e., the "git add <file>...") and commit all changes in the working tree via "git commit -a -m <message>" with -a (or --all) option.

STAGE ALL CHANGES (GIT ADD -A)

You can use "git add -A" to stages all changes in the working tree to the staging area.

UNSTAGE A STAGED FILE (GIT RM --CACHED <FILE> / GIT RESET HEAD <FILE>)

Recall that you can use "git add <file>" to stage new files or modified files into the staging area.

To unstage a staged new file, use "git rm --cached <file>".

To unstage a staged modified file, use "git reset head <file>".

UNMODIFIED A MODIFIED FILE (GIT CHECKOUT -- <FILE>)

After a commit, you may have modified some files. You can discard the changes by checking out the last commit via "git checkout -- <file>".

HOW TO AMEND THE LAST COMMIT (GIT COMMIT --AMEND)

If you make a commit but want to change the commit message:

```
$ git commit --amend -m "message"
```

If you make a commit but realize that you have not staged some file changes, you can also do it with --amend:

```
$ git add morefile
$ git commit --amend
```

You can also make some changes to working tree, stage, and amend the last commit

```
// Edit morefile (make changes)
$ git add morefile
$ git commit --amend
```

How to Undo the Previous Commit(s) (git reset)

To undo previous commit(s):

```
// Reset the HEAD to the previous commit
// --soft to keep the working tree and index
$ git reset --soft HEAD~1    // Windows
$ git reset --soft HEAD^     // Unix

// Make changes
......

// Stage
$ git add ......
// Commit
$ git commit -c ORIG_HEAD
```

The "git reset --hard HEAD~1" moves the HEAD to the previous commit, restore the working tree and discard the index (i.e., discard all change after the previous commit). Instead of HEAD~n, you can also specify the commit hash code.

The "git rest HEAD~1" with default --mixed moves the HEAD to the previous commit, keep the working tree and discard the index

The "git reset --soft HEAD~1" moves the HEAD to the previous commit, keep the working tree and the index (i.e., keep all changes after the previous commit).

For a public repo, you probably need to make another commit and push the commit to the public repo, or ...

RELATIVE COMMIT NAMES

A commit is uniquely and absolutely named using a 160-bit (40-hex-digit) SHA-1 hash code of its contents. You can always refer to a commit via its hash value or abbreviated hash value (such as the first 7 hex-digit) if there is no ambiguity.

You can also refer to a commit relatively, e.g., master~1 (Windows), master^ (may not work in Windows), master^1 refers to the previous (parent) commit on the master branch; master~2, master^^ refers to the previous of the previous (grandparent) commit, and etc. If a commit has multiple parents (e.g., due to merging of branches), ^1 refers to the first parent, ^2 refers to the second parent, and so on.

REFERENCE AND RESOURCES

1. GIT mother site @ http://git-scm.com and GIT Documentation @ http://git-scm.com/doc.
2. Git User's Manual @ http://www.kernel.org/pub/software/scm/git/docs/user-manual.html.
3. Git Hosts: GitHub @ https://github.com, Bitbucket @ https://bitbucket.org.
4. Git Tutorials @ https://www.atlassian.com/git/tutorials.
5. Bitbucket Documentation Home @ https://confluence.atlassian.com/display/BITBUCKET/Bitbucket+Documentation+Home.
6. Bitbucket 101 @ https://confluence.atlassian.com/display/BITBUCKET/Bitbucket+101.
7. Jon Loeliger and Matthew McCullough, "Version Control with Git", 2nd Eds, O'reilly, 2012.
8. Scott Chacon, "Pro Git", Apress, 2009.

www.ingramcontent.com/pod-product-compliance
Lightning Source LLC
Chambersburg PA
CBHW060943050326
40689CB00012B/2563
* 9 7 8 1 9 8 7 5 4 3 8 0 3 *